happy thoughts

happy thoughts

inspiring lessons for a contented life

edited by toby reynolds

Published in the United States in 2007
by Tangent Publications
an imprint of
Axis Publishing Limited
8c Accommodation Road
London NW11 8ED
www.axispublishing.co.uk

Creative Director: Siân Keogh
Editorial Director: Anne Yelland
Production Manager: Jo Ryan

ISBN 978–1–904707–14–1

4 6 8 10 9 7 5 3

Printed and bound in Thailand

about this book

Happy Thoughts brings together an inspirational selection of powerful and life-affirming phrases that have in one way or another helped people to live happier lives, and combines them with evocative and gently amusing animal photographs that bring out the full humor and pathos of the human condition.

We all get down in the dumps sometimes, feel demotivated, and lose confidence in ourselves. These inspiring examples of wit and wisdom, written by real people based on their own true-life experiences, enable us to focus on the important things in life and rediscover our love of life. As one of the entries so aptly puts it—happiness is not a destination; it is a method of life.

So don't worry, be happy!

about the author

Toby Reynolds is an experienced editor ans author who has been involved in book publishing for more than a decade. From the many hundreds of contributions that were sent to him, he has selected the ones that best sum up what a happy life is all about—our relationships, success, and personal well-being.

My natural state is happy.

The grand essentials
of happiness are:
something to do,
something to love,
and something to
hope for.

After years of thinking the
secret of happiness was somehow
eluding me, I realized it was in
what I did and who I cared
for every day.

The secret of happiness
is not to expect.

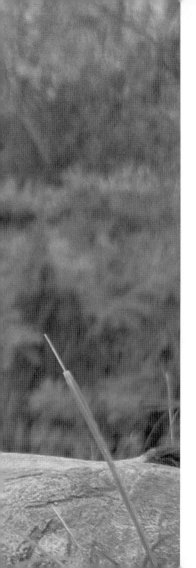

In order to live
freely and happily
you must sacrifice
boredom.

To find out what
one is fitted to do,
and to secure an
opportunity to do it,
are the keys to
happiness.

I realized that the easiest way
to enjoy life is to enjoy what you
do every day—not dream
of escaping it.

Live joyfully and peacefully,
knowing that right thoughts
and right efforts inevitably
bring about right results.

The doors we open
and close each day
decide the lives we live.

Do what you can,
with what you have,
where you are.

Welcome anything that comes to you, but do not long for anything else.

After longing for things
I couldn't have, I thought long and
hard and finally saw that I was
happy with what I'd got.

My riches consist
not in the extent
of my possessions,
but in the fewness
of my wants.

Real riches are
the riches
possessed inside.

Believe that life is worth
living and your belief
will help create the fact.

Forget regret,

or life is yours to miss.

Be true to your work, your word, and your friend.

Being honest all the time
means being happier with yourself
and everything in life.

If you are patient
in one moment
of anger, you will
escape a hundred
days of sorrow.

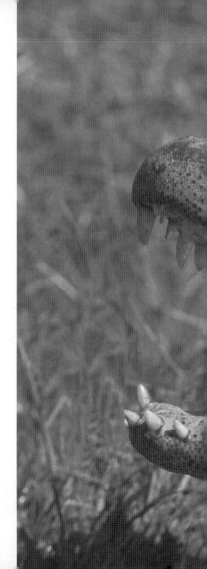

Never look down on anybody unless you are helping him up.

Being kind to others is almost the greatest kindness you can do for yourself as well.

When you are content to be simply yourself and don't compare or compete, everybody will respect you.

Where there is love, there is life.

When I fell in love,
I started to live like
I'd never lived before.

When I find myself fading,
I close my eyes and realize
my friends are my energy.

Nobody really needs to be lonely
or face things alone—it's a habit,
and a very bad one too.

They may forget
what you said, but
they will never
forget how you
made them feel.

The best way to cheer yourself up is to try to cheer somebody else up.

Laughter is
the shortest
distance between
two people.

If you don't learn to laugh at troubles, you won't have anything to laugh at when you grow old.

Nobody ever died
of laughter.

Nurture your mind with great thoughts.

Once you learn the joy
of reading, a whole world of
discovery opens up and you'll
never look back.

There is much pleasure
to be gained from
useless knowledge.

Somewhere, something incredible is waiting to be known.

The most beautiful thing we can experience is the mysterious.

Use what talent you possess; the woods would be very silent if no birds sang except those that sang best.

Everybody should look inside themselves for the thing they can do well and they'll be amazed at the happiness they discover.

Teachers open the door, but you must enter by yourself.

Creative minds have always been known to survive any kind of bad training.

Practice is the best of all instructors.

Never be put off because you
can't do something the
first time—that
happens to everybody.
Never give up; just keep trying.

Don't let life discourage you; everyone who got where he is had to begin where he was.

Without a struggle,
there can be no progress.

Learn to embrace
challenges because they
are a gift in life and not a
difficulty to be avoided.

One that would have the fruit
must climb the tree.

Success in almost any field depends more on energy and drive than it does on intelligence.

To accomplish great things, we must not only act, but also dream; not only plan, but also believe.

All men who have achieved great things have been great dreamers.

When I really believe in my dreams, I find they come true.

Don't be afraid to
take a big step.

You can't cross a chasm
in two small jumps.

Confidence is the hinge on the door to success.

When you learn to
believe in yourself, your
world will open up to you
and you will find your path.

Only those who dare to
fail greatly can ever
achieve greatly.

Freedom is not worth having if it does not include the freedom to make mistakes.

Our greatest glory is
not in never falling,
but in rising every time we fall.

Success seems to be largely a matter of hanging on after others have let go.

It's always too early to quit.

Things that matter in life
always require effort; anything
that matters will never be
that easy, so enjoy it and you
will achieve.

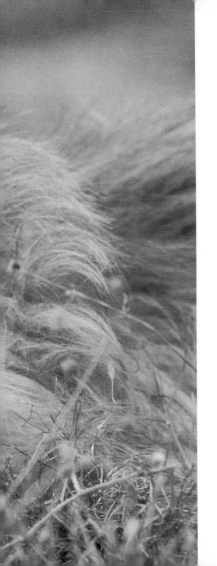

One thing you
can't recycle is
wasted time.

Let him who would enjoy a good future waste none of his present.

He who controls the past
commands the future.

He who commands the future
conquers the past.

The future belongs to
those who believe in the
beauty of their dreams.

I say this to myself whenever
I face frustrations; it pulls me
through, puts a smile on my face,
and helps me achieve my goals.

Go confidently in the direction
of your dreams.

Live the life you have imagined.

Someone who
aims at nothing is
sure to hit it.

There are no shortcuts to
any place worth going.

A journey of a
thousand miles
begins with a
single step.

Even if you are on the right track, you'll get run over if you just sit there.

There are many ways of going forward, but only one way of standing still.

Be happy and it will give you the energy to get what you want in life.

People take different roads
seeking fulfillment
and happiness.

Just because they're not on
your road doesn't mean
they've gotten lost.

I may not have gone where
I intended to go, but I think
I have ended up where
I intended to be.

It is good to have
an end to journey
toward, but it is the
journey that
matters in the end.

The journey
is the reward.

The way to be happy is to
take pleasure in what you do
and how you do it, not in
imagining that happiness is some
place at the end of the road.

Happiness is not a destination;
it is a method of life.